TALES OF AHMEDNAGAR

TALES OF AHMEDNAGAR

CECIL COWLEY

Published by

FacsiMile Publisher
12 Pragati Market
Ashok Vihar, Ph-2
Delhi - 110052, India
Phone: 011-47034999
Email: www.facsimilepublishers.com
info@facsimilepublishers.com

Distribution Network
gyanbooks.com
India, USA, Canada, UK, Australia

ISBN: 978-93-3340-704-5 (PB)

First Published, 1919

2nd Impression 2026

Printed at: Gyan Press, Delhi.

TALES OF AHMEDNAGAR
Author: CECIL COWLEY

TALES
OF
AHMEDNAGAR

BY

CAPTAIN CECIL COWLEY, M.C.
2nd GARRISON BATTALION, NORTHUMBERLAND FUSILIERS

THACKER & COMPANY, LIMITED
BOMBAY

1919

INDEX

INTRODUCTION

On my arrival at Ahmednagar I was much impressed by its noble fort, and was curious to learn its history. I asked questions. The replies were vague and fanciful. I have now made some slight research, and have found very interesting the life of the Deccan Queen, Chand Bibi, contemporary of Queen Elizabeth, and also the other simple tales narrated here. As no work of this nature has hitherto been published, and the facts are undoubtedly of local interest, I have been induced to place them in bookform. For my facts, I have relied largely on the "Bombay Gazetteer," which refers freely to the history by Ferishta, written at Bijapur (A. D. 590-600).

I have also referred to Meadows Taylor's books, kindly lent to me by the Regimental Munshi. For the photographs, I am indebted to Mr. A. C. Wild, I.C.S., Bijapur.

AHMEDNAGAR, CECIL COWLEY.

14th December, 1918.

CHAPTER I

EARLY HISTORY

The Sign Post outside Ahmednagar Post Office indicates the road to Paithan, an almost ruined city and fort about 50 miles distant.

In the era before Christ, Paithan was the capital of the kings of the Andhabritya Dynasty, who ruled the Deccan.

Greek Chroniclers refer to " Paithani " as fine silks and muslins to which the city early gave its name. The industry still exists there, but the manufacture of the modern material is principally carried on at Poona.

In the neighbourhood of Paithan are the hewn caves of Ellora, which are the finest of their kind in the world. They exceed in size and number the Elephanta Caves at Bombay. It has been established by rock inscriptions that the caves date back to about 240 B.C. Other inscriptions record that some of the pillars were the gift of two men of Paithan, one of whom was the king's physician.

Ahmednagar City was not founded till 1494, but for several hundred years before then, the country around was the home of a people, the outlines of whose history has reached us.

It is said that the city of Bhingar, about two miles outside Ahmednagar, is almost as ancient as Paithan, and this may be true, as it is on the caravan route from Paithan, and is situated on a stream which bears its name, and is about two days' journey from Paithan.

Following the Andhrabhrityas, came two successions of the Rashtrakuta kings, who ruled from about A.D. 400 to 973, with a break from 550—670, and gave their names to Maharashtra and the Mahrattas. The caves at Parner and elsewhere with their excellent workmanship and inscriptions, are attributed to their period, and also ancient coins found at Nasik. Govind III. was one of their kings and was a mighty ruler over immense territory.

Chaluky kings reigned from 550-670, and again from 973-1190, and to their period belong the caves and temple at Harishchandrayad in Akola.

They were succeeded by the Deogiri Yadavas, who were invaded and conquered by the Mahomedans, under Mohamed Tuglak in 1294. For a great many years the country was then ruled by Mahomedan Dynasties, and under them attained splendour and power.

CHAPTER II

LAST OF THE YADAVS

One of the last kings to rule before the Mahomedan invasion of the Deccan was Ramchandra, 1271-1310, who was contemporary with Edward I.

A book written in 1290 by a Brahman saint is still preserved and refers to Ramchandra in the following words: "At Niwas . . . . there is a ruler of the earth Ramchandra, who is an ornament to the Yadav Race, the abode of all arts, and the supporter of Justice." The city of Niwas is to-day known as Nevasa, and is 35 miles north of Ahmednagar. Ramchandra's prime minister was an able administrator named Hemadri, who was of Persian origin, andwas an engineer of considerable skill. Scattered over the District there still exist twenty-six "Hemadpanti" walls and temples built and named after him. They are made of huge blocks of stone, placed upon each other without any mortar, and defy the ravages of time.

CHAPTER III

THE TUGLAKS

At first the Mahomedan emperors, who were already established at Delhi, were content to accept tribute from the kings of the Deccan. As, however, this tribute was not regularly paid, Ala-ud-din's general Malikkafur proceeded several times to enforce payment at the point of the sword. He led several campaigns with this object, and succeeded in placing Mahomedan garrisons in many of the chief forts and towns, and finally took up his own residence at Devgiri. The Devgiri Yadavs, however, fought on spiritedly for many years, and on Malikkafur being recalled to Delhi during Ala-ud-din's last illness in 1318, they rose in a well-organised revolt, in which they almost recovered Maharashtra, driving out many garrisons. Ala-ud-din's son then took the field personally, and succeeding in capturing and flaying alive the last of the resisting chiefs. Governors were appointed from Delhi for a time, and in 1338 Ala-ud-din's grandson Mohamed Tuglak, then Emperor of Delhi, came to the Deccan with a vast quantity of elephants, material, nobles and their women, and established his Court at Devgiri, the name of which he changed to Daulatabad, or the Abode of Wealth. He built the cemetery of saints called Roza at Khuldabad, just outside Daulatabad, where Aurangzebe, the last of the Delhi sovereigns to reign in Ahmednagar, was buried in 1707. Daulatabad is not far from Paithan.

After a while Tuglak considered the security of his Court to be doubtful and took it back to Delhi.

CHAPTER IV

THE AFGHAN SOLDIER.

For a period of 50 years or so after the first Mahomedan invasion there was great unrest in the Deccan. For centuries the wealth of the country had been increasing. Gold and precious stones had been amassed by the wealthier classes and the nobility, and there was a plentiful supply of fine and richly wrought clothing and ornaments. The Mahomedan conquerors did not scruple to use the fruits of conquests to the full. They plundered and laid waste the land. Their exactions, instead of leading to a subdued spirit in their newly acquired territories, tended to maintain a spirit of discontent and non-acquiescence.

Among the Delhi troops was an Afghan named Hasan. He had been born in Delhi, the capital of the Empire, and being of very low rank, became a soldier in the natural course of events. As was the custom in those days, he was also a tiller of the soil, and had farmed a plot of land which he rented from a friend of the Emperor. One day he had accidentally found a treasure in the land, and had the honesty to report it to his landlord, a Brahmin named Gangu, who rewarded his honesty by using his interest at court for the advancement of the soldier. By aid of this interest, and his own ability, Hasan rose to considerable station in the Deccan, and his character and love of fair-play inclined him to join a movement to cast aside the misrule of the Delhi authorities, and to restore law and order. His merit singled him out as a leader, and assisted by a number of other Mahomedans, and by the nobles of the Deccan, he was successful in his attempt. He established a government, and treated local chiefs and authorities in a fair and friendly way. He granted a measure of independence to the Koli chiefs, so long as they remained quiet. It is said of one of these chiefs, Paperakoli, of Jawah, that his yearly revenue was nine lakhs of rupees. Gradually the greater portion of Maharastra came under Hasan's influence. He assumed the title of king, and the name Gangu Bahamani, in honour of the astrologer who had first assisted his fortunes. The reign of Ala-ud-din Hasan Gangu Bahamani lasted only 12 years, (1347-1358), but he was succeeded by his son, and subsequently by eighteen other kings of his line, known as the Bahamani kings. Under this dynasty the country prospered. The bandits who had for ages harassed the trade of the Deccan were suppressed, and the people enjoyed peace and good government.

CHAPTER V

THE KINGDOM OF AHMED NIZAM

Towards the latter end of the 15th century the Bahamani kings had their capital at Beedur. Their kingdom was mainly ruled by a number of governors, who exercised authority on their behalf. The four largest provinces of the kingdom had their centres at Bijapur, Berar, Daulatabad and Golkonda, and the great authority vested in the governors of these places, became a source of weakness to their kingdom. In 1480 the prime minister, a man named Mahomed Gawan, proposed a scheme to the king to remedy this. His plan was to subdivide each of the great provinces into two, to leave only one fort in the hands of the governor of each province, and to garrison and officer the other forts direct from the capital, and to pay these garrisons direct from headquarters. Such a system would undoubtedly have destroyed the power of the four great governors. They were filled with alarm at the prospect, and managed to induce the king to have Gawan put to death (1481). He was succeeded as prime minister by Nizam-ul-Mulk Bhairi, a man of great ability, who had had a curious history. His original name was Timapa, and he was the son of a Brahmin village accountant, and was taken prisoner during a punitive expedition, and brought as a slave to Mohamed Shah Bahamani I., the father of the present king. His royal master was so struck with his abilities that he made him playmate to his son, and allowed him to be educated and reared with him, and on Mohamed Shah Bahamani II. ascending the throne, Timapa had taken his place as a great man in the kingdom. He had a military command, and was granted large estates in the district stretching from Poona to Daulatabad, and covering the area of modern Ahmednagar. As he had reached manhood he had adopted the Mahomedan faith, and been given the name Nizam-ul-Mulk Bhairi, the latter being his father's name.

On being appointed prime minister, he sent his son Ahmed to manage his estates, and nominated to the governorship of Daulatabad, two brothers, Malikwaji and Malekashraf, from whom he exacted promises of fidelity to his son Ahmed. These brothers are referred to in the next chapter. In 1486 Nizam-ul-Mulk was assassinated, and his son assumed his father's titles under the name of Ahmed-Nizam-ul-Mulk Bhairi, and remained in his country estates, which he administered with great ability. He rapidly obtained a reputation as a general and as a civil administrator. In 1489 the governors of Bijapur and Berar declared themselves independent kings, and the king of the Bahamanis became anxious to reduce the power of Ahmed, who in the meantime had attacked and captured Shivna, and had secured to himself 5 years' revenue of Maharastra, together with all the places of greatest strength in West and South-West Poona. A general named Shaik Movallid Arab was first sent against him, but his forces were routed by Ahmed near Paranda, and all his elephants, heavy baggage and tents were taken by Ahmed back to Junna. A second

Bahamani force was then despatched against Ahmed, who avoided a general action, but by a flank movement with 3,000 horse, captured the camp of the rearguard at Bedar, and seized all the women of the officers of the Bahamani force. These women he treated with proper respect, and took them to his fortress at Paranda. As a result of his courteous conduct, many of the officers of the Bahamani army declined to fight further against Ahmed, and on his sending the women back, the officers withdrew from action. At the same time, the governor of Paranda also withdrew from the Bahamani army, and sent his son to join Ahmed, who took up a position in the hills about 10 miles west of modern Ahmednagar. Jahangir Khan, the general commanding the Bahamani forces, marched to Bhingar, two miles from Ahmednagar, where he was overtaken by the rains. During the continuance of the rains, Jahangir Khan and his army, fancying themselves secure, gave themselves up to luxury and pleasure. On 28th May, 1490, Ahmed, being well informed of the state of affairs in his enemy's army, made a forced night march, and suddenly attacked his camp at day-break. The attack was completely successful. The Bahamani troops were utterly routed. Many officers of distinction were slain. Others were taken prisoners, and after being led about on buffaloes in Ahmed's triumphal march, they were sent as prisoners to Bedar. Ahmed gave thanks for his victory and built a palace and laid out a garden on the site of the battle, which was thereafter called the Victory of the Garden. During the same year Ahmed reduced Dauda Rajapur in the Central Konkan, and thereby secured unbroken communication between his Deccan territories and the sea coast. His power and dominions were now so great that his people urged him to take upon himself the title of king, and in 1490 he did so, and his name was read in the public prayers. His capital was still at Junna.

CHAPTER VI

THE FOUNDING OF AHMEDNAGAR

King Ahmed, by ceaseless activity and able administration, and by guile, threat and force, consolidated his kingdom. After the Victory of the Garden, he had felt that it would be well for him to cement more firmly to himself the brothers Malik Waji and Malik Ashraf whom his father had appointed to the governorship of Daulatabad, the ancient capital of the Moghuls which was only a little more than 100 miles from Junna and was in a position to render insecure the east of his territory. With this end in view, he gave his sister Bibi Zanat in marriage to Malik Waji, and in due course a son was born. Malik Ashraf, however, was desirous of establishing a kingdom for himself, and in order to avoid counter-claimants, assassinated both his brother and his son, the nephew of Ahmed, and proclaimed himself king of Daulatabad. Bibi Zanat escaped back to her brother, who vowed vengeance against Malik Ashraf, and for many years devoted himself to the fulfilling of the punishment. In 1490 and 1494 he marched against the fort and besieged it, but raised the siege each time.

By this time he realised that the neighbourhood of the Victory of the Garden was of great strategical value. The country around was open, fertile, and free from jungle, and the position commanded the passes from Kandesh, Gujarat and Berar into Central Deccan. He selected a site close by between two rivers, and decided to found his capital there. It was commenced late in 1494. He built a fort and several palaces, and called the place Ahmednagar, or the fort of Ahmed. Such was the success and *éclat* of the new king, that his capital grew apace, and according to Ferishta, the great Ahmednagar historian, within two years of the founding of the city, it was equal in splendour to either Baghdad or Cairo.

Ahmed's chief object at this time was the punishment of the murderer Malik Ashraf, and twice a year Ahmed sent his armies, at the early and late harvests, to lay waste his crops and besiege the fortress of Daulatabad. Finally in 1499 the soldiery in the fort decided to surrender to Ahmed, and on hearing this Malik Ashraf fell ill and died. Ahmed then placed his own garrison in the city, and added its territories to his own.

Ahmed died in 1508. He had once built a tomb for himself in the Roza or Cemetery of Saints at Khuldabad outside Daulatabad, founded by the Emperor Tagluk, but learning that permission would be denied for his burial there, he built another tomb for himself a few hundred yards outside the Nalegaon gate of Ahmednagar, and called it the Bagh Roza. This tomb is at the present day one of the finest of the buildings of the city, and is again referred to in Chapter X.

Ahmed was a great man. His life deserves to be kept in memory. The way in which he quietly and firmly established his kingdom, placed him on a level with the great Afghan soldier from whose dynasty he seceded. He is reported to have been a quiet man, of great continence, kindness and modesty, and firm and strong. He was also a great swordsman, administrator and general, and by these qualities commanded and kept the allegiance of his nobles, of the foreigners who served under him, and also of his sturdy Mahratta peasantry, who made such excellent soldiers.

CHAPTER VII

THE FIRST SIEGE

Burhan Nizam Shah, 1508-1553, was the second king of Ahmednagar. He was endowed with much political sagacity, and was an able general. His Court contained many Turks, Arabs, Persians, and Central Asians. Following on the fall of the Bahamani dynasty, there was much international intrigue in Central and Southern India, and there was constant campaigning, as many as four or five different armies being in the field at one time. Burhan was drawn into the vortex, but successfully steered his kingdom till the end of his long reign of 45 years. In 1525 he three times beat armies of Bahadur Shah, a mighty king of Gujarat, but Bahadur was too strong to accept defeat, and personally marched against Burhan who retreated to Junna, leaving Bahadur to lay siege to the fort of Ahmednagar which then consisted of mud and stone. For three months Burhan from a position in the hills, harrassed the besiegers of the fort, which held out, but ultimately Burhan sued for peace, and the Gujarat king raised the siege and withdrew, leaving the fort intact.

CHAPTER VIII

THE SECOND SIEGE

These were indeed stirring days. As in the Occidental world, great wars and events were taking place, so too in India. There was much marching and counter-marching. Elephants were used in vast numbers, cannons were made by the thousand. There were many tens of thousands of matchlock-men, armed with the ancient type of long-barrelled matchlock, but their number was exceeded still by the number of archers and swordsmen, armed with swords of curious types. The sturdy peasantry were industrious tillers of the soil, and there has rarely been a period of greater agricultural prosperity. But they were all trained to the use of arms, and war was second nature to them. The nobles indulged in sword practice as a pastime, duelling was common, and the ordeal of single combat was still a recognised method of settling disputes. Many people were skilled in the reading and writing of various languages, and there were many learned men. Architecture was on a high level. Magnificent buildings were being erected everywhere. Under the domes and minarets of the Juma Mosque in Bijapur, sister-city to Ahmednagar, six thousand men could kneel in prayer under one roof, and in the same city was then completed the dome of the mausoleum of Sultan Mahomed (nowadays commonly known as the Ibrahim Roza, the glory of the architecture of the Deccan,) which huge structure is second only to the Pantheon in outward diameter. During his reign King

Ahmed I. was engaged in 21 campaigns, his son Burhan I. fought 18 campaigns, and his son Husain nine campaigns. In 1559 during the latter's reign, the kingdom was subjected to a formidable invasion by a combination of three armies, those of Ram Raja, the warrior king of Vijaynagar, of Ibrahim Kutub Shah, the king of Golkonda, and of Ali Adil Shah, the king of Bijapur. Husain, whose generals had hitherto been everywhere victorious, looked for further strength in an alliance with Imad-ul-Mulk, the king of Berar, to whom he made overtures, and to whom he married his daughter. The three allied sovereigns in the meantime reached Ahmednagar, to which they laid siege. Their armies were vast, and according to the translation of Ferishta's History by Major-General Briggs, their

Infantry alone numbered 900,000 men. Husain, however, was not inside the fort, and was at large with the major portion of his army and established his head-quarters at Paithan, whence he got into communication with Kutb Shah, the king of Golkonda, one of the besiegers who, jealous of the Bijapur king's army, convived at passing supplies to the garrison, which was exceedingly strong. Kutb Shah eventually quarrelled with both his allies, and withdrew his army, and returned to Golkonda with a promise of Husain's second daughter in marriage, leaving only two enemies for Husain to deal with. Imudul-Mulk, Husain's new son-in-law, sent a large force to assist him, and he was able to so thoroughly cut off the besiegers' supplies and harass their forces, that they were glad to conclude a peace with him, under which he made certain concessions, the chief of which was the cession of the fortress of Kalliani to Bijapur.

CHAPTER IX

FORT BUILT OF STONE: THIRD AND FOURTH SIEGES.

The fort of Ahmednagar had thus fortunately escaped inviolate from its second siege. And its good fortune was in great measure due to the political and military sagacity of the king, as well as his great strength. Husain resolved to at once make this fort impregnable, and commenced to build it of stone, and to surround it with a deep ditch. The work was commenced in 1559 and was practically completed by 1562, but was improved in later years. Husain was fortunate in his design in having at his Court two great men, Salabat Khan—architect, engineer, general political administrator and reformer, and Chulbi

Rumi Khan, General and Master of Ordinance. He was also in close touch with the Portuguese who had established a Colony at Revandra, at the edge of his dominions, and was in his task assisted by their advice.

As time wore on, Husain chafed under the compulsory cession of the fortress of Kalliani, and in 1562 endeavoured to retake it from Bijapur. Ali Adil Shah at once recalled Ram Raja to his aid, and also obtained the assistance of the kings of Bedar and Berar in punishing the disturber of the peace. Husain, with 700 guns and 500 cannon, marched to meet them, but heavy rain fell and rendered his cattle and guns useless, and he was forced to retreat, taking with him only 40 out of the 700 guns. He threw supplies into the fort of Ahmednagar, and withdrew to Junna, where he rallied and reformed his army. The allies in the meantime laid siege to the fort and followed Husain. After several weeks the allies found that Husain's army was attaining such strength that they withdrew the investing forces from the fort to assist in an action against Husain. The fort thus escaped uncaptured from its third siege. Husain, however, avoided a general action. In several minor engagements he inflicted loss on the allies, and on the rains of 1563 setting in, the allies returned to Ahmednagar and settled down to its fourth siege, the main portion of Ram Rajah's army being to the south of the fort, on the bank of the Sina River. During the night heavy rain fell in the hills, and the river came down in flood so suddenly that it swept away 25,000 of Ram Raja's men, 300 horses, and practically the whole of his transport. The allies, disturbed by this disaster, and considering the new fort to be wellnigh impregnable, determined to raise the siege, (the fourth), and withdrew their armies. The fort was not again invested by neighbouring states until the Moghuls marched against Queen-Regent Chand Bibi, but it was a factor of importance in many subsequent internal disturbances.

Photo of the front portion of Malek-i-Maidan (Master of the Plain) at present mounted on a bastion of the Fort at Bijapur. This is the largest piece of cast brass ordnance in the world, and was made at Ahmednagar about 1550.

CHAPTER X

THE LARGEST GUN IN THE WORLD

Among the foreigners who entered king Burhan's service was a Turk named Chulbi Rumi Khan, who was an expert artillery man, skilled in the manufacture and use of cannon. In the reign of king Burhan, he made two enormous cannons, the larger of the two being named "Malik-i-Madan" (Master of the Plain) and the second "Dhuldan" —or "Destroyer." These cannon were cast in the garden outside the tomb of Chulbi Rumi Khan in Ahmednagar, and a large depression in the garden is still pointed out as being the site where they were moulded. The larger of the two weighs 40 tons, and is the largest piece of cast brass ordnance in the world.

They were lost by King Husain in 1562 in the battle before the third siege of Ahmednagar, when owing to the difficulty of movement in the wet clay Husain abandoned them together with 700 other guns and 500 elephants to Ali Adil Shah of Bijapur and Ram Raja. Malik-i-Maidan was dragged by elephants to Bijapur, and mounted on a bastion of the fort, where it remains to this day, a much prized trophy, and proof of the prowess of the nation. Dhuldan met with a less splendid fate. It was capsized in the River Krishna, near Bijapur, where it can still be seen when the water is low.

In 1553 Chulbi Rumi Khan had been advanced to the command of an army which moved against the Portugese fort and settlement. The campaign was successful, the

Portuguese promising not to molest or encroach on Ahmednagar's dominions.

After the severe losses of 1562 and 1563, Khan, as Master of the King's Ordnance, devoted all his energies to the creation of fresh Artillery, and the whole kingdom roused itself to effort, the king and Court being guided by his mature experience and advice.

In two years time, five hundred brass cannon were cast in Ahmednagar.

CHAPTER XI

A DECISIVE BATTLE

King Husain realised the futility of fighting against so strong a combination as that which had operated against him in 1562-63, especially when the heart and soul of the combine was a strong and astute monarch and general such as Ram Raja, king of Vijaynagar. By clever diplomacy he regained the sympathy of his son-in-law, the king of Golkonda, and also that of the king of Bedar. He also entered into an alliance with Ali Adil Shah, king of Bijapur, to whom he gave his beautful daughter, the Princess Chand Bibi, in marriage. This union he further strengthened by a marriage between Ali Adil Shah's sister Princess of Bijapur and Murtaza, Prince Royal of Ahmednagar.

In 1564 Ram Raja decided to again invade Ahmednagar, and moved against it with an army of 70,000 cavalry, 90,000 infantry, chiefly armed with matchlocks, and a large force of artillery and archers.

Husain called for and received the support of the kings of Golkonda, Berar and Bijapur and their forces, and the allies marched to meet Ram Raja.

The armies approached each other near the Hukeri River, south of the Krishna.

Ram Raja had a certain amount of moral ascendancy over the kings of Bijapur and Bedar, both of whom had previously served with him. He was also held in fear by Golkonda, whose forces had fled from him the previous year. Husain also did not under-estimate him as he had previously had him as adversary.

The allies therefore, on the near approach of battle, gave pause, reconsidered their position, and came to the conclusion that they were unable to cope with their enemy, skilled as he was, and supported by such formidable forces.

They thereupon made overtures of peace, but Ram Raja refused to listen to their offers, and the allies, of whom Husain was the strongest in character, resolved to fight to the death. The allies were all Mahomedan kings. Their enemy was Hindoo, and it appeared that the supremacy of Mahomedanism as well as the temporal power of the allied kings was at stake. The armies therefore placed themselves in battle array. Ahmednagar decided to take the post of honour in the centre of the line, with Ali Adil Shah on his right, and Bedar and Golkonda on his left.

Expecting to receive the weight of the attack in the centre, Husain entrusted the command of his guns and the disposition of his forces to Chulbi Rumi Khan. This astute artilleryman following the device recently adopted by the king of Sweden in the European wars, covered his front with his artillery, 300 pieces in all, which he placed in three lines—the smallest in front, the medium sized in the middle, and the largest behind—a wise plan, as rapid loading was then unknown. To make the fire of the guns deadly, he loaded each with hundreds of copper coins, and had the fuses of the whole ready to be lighted at a word of command. He further covered his artillery by a strong force of archers, and awaited the advance of the enemy.

Ram Raja moved to the attack. The defending archers maintained a heavy discharge as he approached. On the enemy arriving close, the archers withdrew, and disclosed the front line of guns which let go their murderous charges at close range. The front line of gunners then withdrew, and the second line of guns was discharged with deadly effect. Their gunners withdrew, and the third line of guns was instantly fired. The slaughter in the ranks of the enemy was terrific. The attack was broken, and the allies' horse and foot, charged into the masses of Hindoos, who broke and fled utterly routed leaving vasty booty in the hands of the allies. Ram Raja was overtaken by an officer mounted on an elephant. The elephant seized him in its trunk, and he was carried prisoner to the allied kings, who immediately had him beheaded and Ram Rajah's head and body were taken to Ahmednagar. His skull was preserved, and is still treasured in the little city of Bhingar by the descendants of his executioner, and his tomb at Ahmednagar is still in good repair.

The driver of the elephant was buried beside the tomb of Ahmed I. in the Bagh Roza, and his grave is denoted by a monument resembling a howdah.

The elephant on its death was also honoured by burial just outside the Bagh Roza, and its grave is still distinguished by a mound of earth.

CHAPTER XII

GREAT MEN

King Husain died after the Battle of the Hukeri, and was succeeded by his son Murtaza Nizam Shah (1564-1588) whose reason appeared to become slightly affected as he aged. The kingdom, however, was fortunate in possessing at this time several men of great intellect and administrative ability, and the country under their guidance was maintained for a few years at the pinnacle of prosperity and power to which it attained in Husain's day.

CHANGIZ KHAN.

Changiz Khan, a noble of Turkish origin, was a minister and general of great integrity and attachment to the throne, and managed public affairs for some time. The king, however, filled with suspicion, prescribed a draught of poisoned medicine for him, which he quietly accepted and drank in his own home. The palace he built and occupied in the city is still in good repair, and is now used as the District Judge's Court.

SALABAT KHAN.

Salabat Khan (1519-1589), to whom reference has already been made, was also one of the greatest men of the Nizam Shah dynasty. Born in 1518, he was of good family, and served his apprenticeship in the Court of Burhan. He early proved himself an expert engineer and architect, and was at the height of his profession when the fort was built of stone, and no doubt took a considerable part in its construction. The building of the pleasure palace of Farah Bag, just outside the city, at one time entrusted to his uncle, Salabat Khan I. by Burhan I., was finally completed by the nephew, who erected a number of other palaces and public buildings, both within and without the fort. His chief usefulness, however, lay in the large public works instigated by him. He cut seven large aqueducts to bring water to the city and fort from perennial supplies in the hills. In some places these aqueducts were carried 60 ft. underground. Four of them, with slight alterations, are used for supplying the modern city and cantonment with water. Over a million fruit trees are said to have been planted by him throughout the kingdom. He took office under Murtaza, and in his reign became Minister without a rival, and continued in power for several years, it being popularly said that the kingdom had never been so well governed for over a hundred years.

Murtaza was a difficult king to serve. At one time he suffered from religious enthusiasm, at another was overwhelmed with remorse and lived in privacy, and at other times he sought the companionship of profligates. At one period he had as favourite, a dancing girl to whom he gave grants of land and gifts of royal jewels. At last he ordered the two most valuable necklaces from Ram Raja's plunder to be given to the girl, but Salabat Khan, unwilling that such priceless gems should be lost to the royal family, tried to prevent it. The king, in a paroxysm of rage threw the whole lot into a large fire. He again crossed the king when the latter, suspicious of the heir-apparent, attempted to put him to death.

Eventually the king upbraided him with treachery, and Salabat Khan immediately begged the king to appoint a place for his confinement, and submitted himself to the king's guards, and was carried to prison, where he remained till the troublous times which followed the king's death. He then emerged for a few months, but was broken in health and spirit and died in 1589 at the age of 70 years, and was buried in a tomb which stands out prominently on the rocky summit of the eastern extremity of a range of hills six miles from Ahmednagar. From this site can be seen great stretches of the country for the material prosperity of which he did so much, and the tomb itself can be seen from many miles around.

FERISHTAH

Ferishtah, the historian, was brought by his father from the Caspian Sea to Murtaza's court while still a young boy. He served there in a military capacity during the troubles which occurred at the end of Murtaza's reign, and finally, with many other foreigners who were expelled from the kingdom, took refuge at the court of Bijapur, where he was favourably received, and where he wrote the famous history, in connection with which he testifies that the king of Bijapur spared no expense in supplying him with materials.

Ferishtah's History narrates many of the facts related in this book.

CHAPTER XIII

CHAND BIBI

Chand Bibi (1550-1594) is the favourite heroine of the Deccan, and is the subject of many legends. Born at Ahmednagar, she was the daughter of King Husain, and the sister of Murtaza and his brother Burhan II., both kings of Ahmednagar. In 1564 she was married to Ali Adil Shah, king of the sisterkingdom of Bijapur, and on his death was regent for four years for his nephew Ibrahim. She was also aunt to Ismail and Ibrahim, kings of Ahmednagar, and was related to many other of the ruling houses of the Deccan. Descendant of a line of able kings, she inherited their intellect and ability. During her married life she was the constant companion of her husband in all his doings, and was present at the battle of the Hukeri, when Ram Raja was defeated and slain. Thereafter during a tour of several years in which her husband was engaged in the settlement and pacification of the territories which had fallen to him under the terms of partition, by her tact and charm she was of great value in securing the loyalty of the Chieftains of the Beydurs and other spirited tribes.

After her husband's death, her personal heroism and generalship during the siege of Bijapur (approx. 1582) undoubtedly saved that city from capture, and in 1590, at the siege of Ahmednagar, her dauntless courage saved the fort from the Moghuls.

Her wisdom and self-reliance, her pure administration and noble deeds in critical days deserve their lasting place in the people's affection.

Of remarkable beauty, she was unblessed by children, and retained her grace of figure until the day of her violent death.

Always elegantly dressed, she used to ride astride on a richly caparisoned steed, whether to the field, on tour, or hunting. In deference to custom, her face used to be slightly concealed by a wisp of some fine material, but she never wore a formal veil.

At Bijapur there is a portrait taken of her by a Persian artist before her husband's death. It is a profile, exquisitely painted in body colour, with none of the stiffness which usually accompanies Oriental pictures. The features are regular and very beautiful. The complexion fair, with a faint tinge of carnation through the cheeks. The eyes blue-grey,

The Deccan Heroine: CHAND BIBI,
Princess of Ahmednagar and Queen of Bijapur.
From an excellent water colour in Bijapur
Museum, Painted about 1585.

with long dark eyelashes. The mouth is very gentle and sweet in expression, and bears a slight smile, but there is a decided tone of firmness about the full round chin and graceful throat, and the forehead has a breadth and power which must have been very remarkable.

Her education proceeded for many years after her marriage, and she became skilled in Persian, Arabic, Turkish and Toorki, and spoke the dialects current in the army with fluency. She drew and painted flowers with ease and delicacy, played upon the *vina* with skill, and had a great many other accomplishments. With her husband, she fostered trade, literature and the arts of peace, and prosecuted those works for the defence and adornment of his capital which still remain as monuments of his enlightened liberality. The city of Bijapur at this period had a population of 1,500,000, and the kingdom was powerful and prosperous.

On her husband's death, her independent political life began as regent for the minor king. In those times it was a rare thing to find nobles, ministers, and generals of a native kingdom true to their allegiance for long, and serious dissensions occurred between powerful factions and encouraged the invasion of the kingdom by the kings of Berar, Beedu and Golconda, and the close investment of the city. The queen, accompanied by her nephew the king, used to go from post to post at night, cheering, encouraging and directing all. The weather was the severest of the rainy season, and after days of drenching rain and bombardment by the enemy, a portion of the city wall gave way. Notwithstanding the torrential downpour.

the queen guarded the breach in person, collected the masons of the city, and personally superintended the work of repair, leaving the spot neither by day nor night till it was safe against attack by storm. Her devotion and spirited personal valour inspired confidence in all, which now amounted to positive enthusiasm. The leaders of the various factions went to her in a body, and submitted themselves to her authority. In less than a month many thousands of the followers of the different nobles were collected under proper command within and without the city, and the besieging armies thought it advisable to raise the siege. It had lasted a year.

By her personality Chand Bibi maintained perfect order till Ibram Adil Shah, the young king, came of age and her regency terminated.

Meanwhile the armies of the Moghuls began to move southwards. Though no act of invasion occurred, the queen became uneasy, and in 1585 Murtaza being king of Ahmednagar, and Salabat Khan his minister, in order to consolidate the two kingdoms, she arranged a marriage between Mirain Hussein, Prince Royal of Ahmednagar, and the sister of Ibrahim Adil Shah. Being aunt to both contracting parties, she decided to accompany the bride-elect to Ahmednagar, her own native town, from which she had been absent for over 20 years. The splendour and pomp of the wedding were magnificent.

King Murtaza, however, was in his dotage, and shortly after her arrival at Ahmednagar occurred the incident of the burning of Ram Raja's jewels, and two attempts on his son's life by the king. The prince thereupon went into rebellion, and the garrison of the fort being favourable to him, he entered it with his troops, and seizing the king, placed him in a bathroom of the fort and had a huge fire lighted under it, so that the king was suffocated by the steam. The new king (Mirain Hussein) proved headstrong, suspicious and cruel. In one day, for fear of treason, he put to death 15 princes of the line of succession. The Queen Chand decided to stay on in Ahmednagar. The threat of the Moghuls was ever present to her vision, and she feared internal political dissension would weaken her two beloved kingdoms, and prove an inducement to invasion.

Mirain Hussein (1588) only reigned for six months. He declared in a fit of drunkenness that he would have his prime minister (a Turk) beheaded, and made plans to do so, but the minister by a clever ruse captured the king and declared him deposed. In the disturbances that followed both the king and the minister were slain. The troops and the mob put to death every foreigner they could find in the fort or the city. The massacre lasted for seven days, and only a few escaped.

Ismail Nizam Shah (1588-1589), nephew of Queen Chand, and son of her brother Burhan, was then declared king. All sorts of factions arose, both political and religious, and the king of Bijapur sent an army to secure safety. Jamal Khan, the strongest man in the kingdom, marched to meet it. For 15 days the two forces lay facing each other without action, and finally a peace was concluded, under which Jamal Khan remained regent, and agreed to pay £850,000 (270,000 huns) to Bijapur. Queen Chand returned to Bijapur.

Burhan (1589-1594), brother of the late King Murtaza, and father of Ismail Nizam Shah, then marched from the north, where for many years he had sheltered under the Moghuls, and wrested the throne from his son. He only lived a short while, and on his death he was succeeded by his son Ibrahim Nizam Shah (1594) who was killed the same year.

On his death the kingdom was in a hopeless state, and was largely split up among the nobles. In the absence of an heir of mature age, different parties nominated different kings.

Mian Manju Dakhani supported the cause of a lad named Ahmad, whom he alleged to be a son of Shah Kassim, second brother of Murtaza.

Another faction supported the claim of Bahadur (an infant in arms), son of Ibrahim

Nizam Shah, and proposed Queen Chand as regent.

Nehang Khan approached Shah Ali, the son of Burhan Nizam Shah I., then upwards of 70 years of age, and induced him to leave his retirement and assume the royal canopy.

In the meantime the Moghuls moved their armies still further south, and awaited an excuse to invade the wealthy country.

CHAPTER XIV

THE FIFTH SIEGE: CHAND BIBI'S DEFENCE

In this condition of chaos, an appeal was made to Queen Chand, to come and use her personal influence and ascendancy in the cause of law and order. She thereupon left the Bijapur court and returned to her palace in Ahmednagar fort (1594) in the hope that she might be able to unite the country.

Malek Umbar, an Abyssinian who had risen from slavery to become Governor of Daulatabad, and who was a shrewd man and a capable administrator, and who had held his hand till he could decide on what would be the best course for the country, welcomed her. A number of other chiefs did the same.

In the meantime Mian Manju had entered into correspondence with Prince Murad, son of the Emperor Akbar, and had invited him to bring the Moghul forces to Ahmednagar. Prince Murad seized the opportunity, and marched on Ahmednagar, laying siege to the fort on 14th December 1594, having with him a vast army of foot and 30,000 cavalry.

Queen Chand had rallied a considerable force. She took command of the defence personally and used daily to inspect the guns, sentries, and troops, and by her calmness and serenity maintained a spirit of confidence in the defenders. She also sent a successful appeal to Mian Manju, Yeklas Khan and Nehang Khan to lay aside their differences for the common cause, and to unite their strength against the invaders. The kings of Golconda and Bijapur also sent assistance at her request, and the friendly forces united their armies. Though they did not advance to attack the Moghuls, they were able to restrict the activities of their foraging parties, and kept them very short of supplies.

The besiegers slowly but methodically closed in on the fort. They advanced by means of saps and trenches and by the night of 19th February, 1596, had laid five mines, which it was their intention to explode at dawn the next morning. During the night, however, the defenders were made aware of the plans of the enemy, and under the personal direction of the queen, began to counter-mine. They discovered and destroyed two of the mines, and were in the act of removing the powder from the largest mine, when Prince Murad gave orders for it to be sprung. A tremendous explosion blew a large breach in the wall of the fort, and put fear into the defenders, who commenced to flee, but the queen, clad in armour, with a veil on her head, and a drawn sword in her hand, leaped into the breach and stayed the panic. The Moghuls did not immediately attack, and the defenders, taking advantage of the delay, hurriedly put the breach into a rough state of defence, and trained on to it all their available artillery, loaded as on a previous occasion, with copper coins. The Moghuls stormed the breach at four o'clock in the afternoon, but the garrison resisted with heroism, inspired by the wonderful example of the queen. Time after time was the attack repeated, and time after time repelled, and it was not till nightfall that the carnage ceased, by which time thousands of dead lay in the ditch. Under cover of the darkness the queen repeated her deed of Bijapur, and personally superintended the repairs to the breach. Working at feverish heat, by dawn she had had the wall rebuilt to a height of seven feet, and felt prepared to resist another attack. But the army of Prince Murad was short of supplies. Daunted by the splendid defence, and harassed by the allied cavalry behind and around him, he made an offer to withdraw his forces provided that Ahmednagar agreed to cede back to the Moghuls the disputed territory of Berar.

At first the queen declined these terms, but on reflection decided that if the allies were beaten in a general action, equally good terms might not again be offered. She therefore signed a treaty in the name of Bahadur, the infant king, and Prince Murad marched away, leaving the fort uncaptured. Historians differ as to the merits of the action of the allies who came to her assistance but only hovered around and failed to attack the Moghuls, but all are agreed in according to the queen the greatest praise for her magnificent defence of the fort.

CHAPTER XV

THE SIXTH SIEGE : CHAND BIBI'S DEATH.

For three years the Queen-Regent ruled the kingdom, but the Moghuls were restless on her borders. One by one the kingdoms of Gujarat, Malwa and Khandesh fell to their arms, and they began to occupy districts much to the south of Berar. The kings of Golconda and Bijapur, assisted by troops from Ahmednagar, gave them battle on the Godavery River. After a bloody general engagement which lasted two days, victory rested with the Moghuls. Queen Chand still hoped that she would be able to induce the Moghuls to abide by their treaty, but to complicate matters Nehang Khan, rash and untrustworthy, went into rebellion against the queen, and laid siege to the town of Bid, which the Moghuls had occupied. This rash action speedily drew the wrath of the Moghuls. Prince Murad being dead, the Emperor Akbar sent his second son, Prince Danyal, to the relief of the city. Nehang Khan fled and sought refuge at Ahmednagar. Queen Chand realised that the Battle of the Godavery and Nehang's action had probably decided the fate of the Nizam Dynasty, but still hoped that by discreet diplomacy she might be able to save it. She refused Nehang Khan admission to the fort, and he fled further. Prince Danyal, however, followed in his wake with a large army and a powerful siege train specially equipped, and manned by skilled and daring miners from the North, and laid siege to the fort, which was again bravely defended by the Queen-Regent. The Emperor Akbar had however set his mind on the reduction of the fort and proceeded to Burhanpur to direct it. Operations were unceasingly pressed forward. Mines were formed from the trenches of the prince, but the besieged broke into them and filled them. One mine was carried under the palace in the fort before being discovered. The queen began to despair of success by arms. The armies of Golconda and Bijapur dare not assist her, and practically no troops were operating on her behalf outside the fort. After four months' gallant defence she came to the conclusion that she could no longer hold the fort, and that it would be policy to surrender it on the condition that the Moghuls allowed her to move with the young king and the garrison to Junna. By this means she hoped to maintain an independent kingdom even without Ahmednagar. On hearing this, Hamid Khan, the commander of the fort, rushed into the streets crying "Treason treason, the queen will betray us." The Dekhanis, wrought to a high pitch of nervous tension by 16 weeks of strain and anxiety, and forgetful of all their past debts to the queen, rushed in a mob to her private apartments, where Hamid Khan cut her down with his drawn sword. Thus ended the life of Chand Bibi, in the palace where she was born. She was doubtless buried within the fort. No tomb marks her grave, but she still lives in the memory of the people, beloved and honoured.

* * * * *

The fort held out only four days longer. On the fourth day several mines were sprung. A huge crack began to show in one bastion. The besiegers placed 180 mans of gunpowder therein, and on it being exploded the bastion and many yards of the wall were thrown into the air. The breach was stormed. Fifteen hundred of the defenders were put to the sword. The guns and ammunition captured were beyond compute and a valuable booty, treasure and jewels fell to the victors. The boy king was taken prisoner, and the Moghuls reigned in Ahmednagar (1599).

CHAPTER XVI

THE SEVENTH SIEGE: MOGHULS, MAHRATTAS AND BRITISH.

Malik Umbar for some years endeavoured to maintain the claims of the Nizam Shah Dynasty to the Ahmednagar Kingdom. Wise and courageous, he to some extent succeeded, but on his death, in the absence of a strong champion or claimant, the kingdom expired. During the century that followed, the Mahratta chieftains in outlying forts began to grow strong and bold. The Emperor Aurangzebe moved his court to Ahmednagar, and died there in 1707, and on his death the dissensions among his sons weakened the Moghul power in the Deccan. In 1716 a bloody battle was fought near Ahmednagar between Khanderav Dabhade, a Mahratti leader, and Husain Ali, of the Moghuls, in which the advantage lay with the Mahrattas, and the fall of the Moghul power was completed in 1748 when the fort and district passed to the Chin Kilich Khan, Nizam-ul-Mulk, Governor of Malwa. In 1759 the fort was betrayed by a bribe of a large sum of money by the Nizam's Commandant to the Mahrattas. There was much fighting in the Deccan, in which French and the East India Company troops participated. In 1795, for services rendered, the Peshwa ceded to his general Daulatrav Scindia, the fort of Ahmednagar and certain lands. In 1802 the British entered into a treaty with the Peshwa for mutual defence. In 1803 Scindia commenced to march against the Peshwa, and on being called on to desist by General Wellesley (afterwards the Duke of Wellington), he cynically advised the General to withdraw to Madras, Seringapatam, or Bombay. Wellesley however moved against Ahmednagar, and on 7th August, 1803, attacked and took the town, which was held by a large number of troops, and then proceeded to invest the fort. He seized a position to the east of the wall, 400 yards distant, and opened fire with a battery of guns. The fire was maintained without pause, and with deadly effect, and after two days' battering, the commander of the fort offered to surrender the fort on condition that the garrison should be allowed to depart with their private property. To this General Wellesley agreed, and on the morning of 12th August, 1803, the garrison marched out and General Wellesley took possession. On marching in he found the fort in excellent repair, with a vast amount of stores and gunpowder of good quality. The interior of the fort was crowded with palaces and buildings, which led to confusion. The General thought they should be removed, and in later days the material taken from these buildings was utilised in the erection of the Wellesley Barracks, to the east of the fort. The fort was handed to the Peshwa, who ceded it to the British under the treaty of Poona, in June 1817. During the Mutinies of 1857, about 7,000 Bhils rose in rebellion; they were suppressed almost entirely by the Police and a special Koli corps: except for this there has been no war in the land. On account of its strategic position the fort has been maintained in good repair, and for over a century it has been garrisoned by British troops. Day by day the 12 o'clock gun booms out from on its stately walls, carrying a message of peace and security to the distant hills.